Chowders and Broths: 50 Savory Soup Recipes

By: Kelly Johnson

Table of Contents

- New England Clam Chowder
- Chicken and Corn Chowder
- Creamy Potato Chowder
- Lobster Bisque
- Tomato Basil Soup
- French Onion Soup
- Beef Barley Soup
- Chicken Noodle Soup
- Split Pea Soup with Ham
- Broccoli Cheddar Soup
- Minestrone Soup
- Roasted Butternut Squash Soup
- Thai Coconut Chicken Soup
- Mushroom and Wild Rice Soup
- Italian Wedding Soup
- Shrimp and Corn Chowder
- Tuscan White Bean Soup
- Seafood Chowder
- Sweet Potato and Carrot Soup
- Roasted Cauliflower Soup
- Creamy Spinach and Artichoke Soup
- Moroccan Chickpea Soup
- Tomato and Red Pepper Bisque
- Curried Lentil Soup
- Chicken Tortilla Soup
- Beef and Vegetable Soup
- Spicy Black Bean Soup
- Pea and Mint Soup
- Pumpkin Soup with Ginger
- Baked Potato Soup
- Chicken and Rice Soup
- Chicken and Wild Rice Soup
- Roasted Garlic and Potato Soup
- Creamy Cauliflower Soup
- Kale and White Bean Soup

- Sweet Corn and Zucchini Soup
- Roasted Beetroot Soup
- Cabbage and Sausage Soup
- Spicy Pumpkin and Lentil Soup
- Italian Sausage and Kale Soup
- Smoky Ham and Potato Soup
- Clam and Bacon Chowder
- Coconut Curry Butternut Squash Soup
- Vietnamese Pho
- Fish Chowder
- Potato Leek Soup
- Eggplant and Tomato Soup
- Chicken and Sweet Potato Soup
- Green Bean and Ham Soup
- Coconut Lentil Soup

New England Clam Chowder

Ingredients:

- 4 cups fresh clams, shucked and chopped
- 4 slices bacon, chopped
- 1 medium onion, diced
- 2 cloves garlic, minced
- 3 medium potatoes, peeled and diced
- 2 cups chicken broth
- 1 cup heavy cream
- 1 cup whole milk
- Salt and freshly ground black pepper to taste
- Fresh parsley, chopped, for garnish

Instructions:

In a large pot, cook the bacon over medium heat until crisp. Remove and set aside, leaving the bacon drippings in the pot. Add the onions and garlic, and sauté until softened, about 5 minutes. Add the diced potatoes, chicken broth, and bring to a simmer. Cook the potatoes until tender, about 10 minutes. Stir in the clams, heavy cream, and milk, and bring to a simmer again. Cook for another 5 minutes, seasoning with salt and pepper to taste. Serve the chowder hot, garnished with crispy bacon and chopped parsley.

Chicken and Corn Chowder

Ingredients:

- 2 cups cooked chicken, shredded
- 2 cups frozen corn kernels
- 1 medium onion, diced
- 2 cloves garlic, minced
- 2 medium potatoes, peeled and diced
- 4 cups chicken broth
- 1 cup heavy cream
- Salt and freshly ground black pepper to taste
- 2 tablespoons butter
- Fresh parsley, chopped, for garnish

Instructions:

In a large pot, melt butter over medium heat. Add the onion and garlic, cooking until softened. Add the potatoes and chicken broth, bringing to a boil. Reduce the heat and simmer until the potatoes are tender, about 10 minutes. Stir in the chicken and corn, and cook for an additional 5 minutes. Pour in the heavy cream and simmer for another 5 minutes. Season with salt and pepper to taste. Garnish with fresh parsley and serve warm.

Creamy Potato Chowder

Ingredients:

- 4 medium potatoes, peeled and diced
- 1 medium onion, diced
- 2 cloves garlic, minced
- 4 cups chicken broth
- 1 cup heavy cream
- 2 tablespoons butter
- Salt and freshly ground black pepper to taste
- Fresh thyme, for garnish

Instructions:

In a large pot, melt butter over medium heat. Add the onion and garlic, sautéing until softened. Add the potatoes and chicken broth, bringing to a boil. Lower the heat and simmer until the potatoes are tender, about 10 minutes. Use an immersion blender to puree the soup until smooth, or transfer to a blender in batches. Stir in the heavy cream, and cook for another 5 minutes. Season with salt and pepper to taste, and garnish with fresh thyme. Serve warm.

Lobster Bisque

Ingredients:

- 2 lobster tails, cooked and chopped
- 1/2 cup butter
- 1 medium onion, diced
- 2 cloves garlic, minced
- 1 cup tomato paste
- 2 cups chicken broth
- 1 cup heavy cream
- 1/4 cup brandy (optional)
- Salt and freshly ground black pepper to taste
- Fresh parsley, for garnish

Instructions:

In a large pot, melt butter over medium heat. Add the onion and garlic, sautéing until softened. Stir in the tomato paste, and cook for 2 minutes. Add the chicken broth and bring to a simmer, cooking for 10 minutes. Stir in the heavy cream and brandy (if using), then bring back to a simmer. Add the lobster meat and cook for another 5 minutes. Season with salt and pepper to taste. Garnish with fresh parsley and serve.

Tomato Basil Soup

Ingredients:

- 6 ripe tomatoes, chopped
- 1 medium onion, diced
- 2 cloves garlic, minced
- 4 cups vegetable broth
- 1 cup fresh basil leaves
- 1 cup heavy cream
- 2 tablespoons olive oil
- Salt and freshly ground black pepper to taste

Instructions:

In a large pot, heat olive oil over medium heat. Add the onion and garlic, cooking until softened. Add the tomatoes and cook until they begin to break down, about 10 minutes. Pour in the vegetable broth and bring to a boil. Reduce the heat and simmer for 15 minutes. Use an immersion blender to puree the soup until smooth, or transfer to a blender. Stir in the basil and heavy cream, and simmer for another 5 minutes. Season with salt and pepper to taste. Serve warm.

French Onion Soup

Ingredients:

- 4 large onions, thinly sliced
- 2 tablespoons butter
- 2 cloves garlic, minced
- 6 cups beef broth
- 1/2 cup dry white wine
- 1 teaspoon fresh thyme, chopped
- 1 tablespoon flour
- Salt and freshly ground black pepper to taste
- 4 slices baguette
- 1 1/2 cups Gruyère cheese, shredded

Instructions:

In a large pot, melt butter over medium heat. Add the onions and cook, stirring occasionally, until caramelized, about 25-30 minutes. Add the garlic and cook for 1 more minute. Stir in the flour and cook for 2 minutes. Add the wine, scraping up any browned bits from the bottom of the pot. Pour in the beef broth and thyme, and bring to a boil. Reduce the heat and simmer for 20 minutes. Season with salt and pepper to taste. To serve, ladle the soup into bowls, top with a slice of baguette, and sprinkle with Gruyère cheese. Broil until the cheese is melted and bubbly.

Beef Barley Soup

Ingredients:

- 1 lb beef stew meat, cubed
- 1 medium onion, diced
- 2 carrots, sliced
- 2 celery stalks, sliced
- 2 cloves garlic, minced
- 6 cups beef broth
- 1 cup pearl barley
- 1 teaspoon dried thyme
- Salt and freshly ground black pepper to taste
- 2 tablespoons olive oil

Instructions:

In a large pot, heat olive oil over medium heat. Add the beef and brown on all sides. Remove the beef and set aside. In the same pot, sauté the onion, carrots, celery, and garlic until softened. Return the beef to the pot, and add the beef broth, barley, and thyme. Bring to a boil, then reduce the heat and simmer for 45 minutes, or until the barley and beef are tender. Season with salt and pepper to taste. Serve warm.

Chicken Noodle Soup

Ingredients:

- 2 cups cooked chicken, shredded
- 2 medium carrots, sliced
- 2 celery stalks, sliced
- 1 medium onion, diced
- 4 cups chicken broth
- 1 cup egg noodles
- 1/2 teaspoon dried thyme
- Salt and freshly ground black pepper to taste
- Fresh parsley, for garnish

Instructions:

In a large pot, sauté the onion, carrots, and celery in a bit of oil until softened. Add the chicken broth and bring to a boil. Stir in the chicken and thyme, then add the egg noodles. Simmer until the noodles are tender, about 10 minutes. Season with salt and pepper to taste. Garnish with fresh parsley before serving.

Split Pea Soup with Ham

Ingredients:

- 2 cups dried split peas, rinsed
- 1 lb ham hock or ham bone
- 1 medium onion, diced
- 2 carrots, sliced
- 2 celery stalks, sliced
- 4 cups chicken broth
- Salt and freshly ground black pepper to taste
- 2 cloves garlic, minced

Instructions:

In a large pot, combine the split peas, ham hock, onion, carrots, celery, garlic, and chicken broth. Bring to a boil, then reduce the heat and simmer for about 1-2 hours, until the peas are soft and the soup is thickened. Remove the ham hock, shred the meat, and return it to the pot. Season with salt and pepper to taste. Serve hot.

Broccoli Cheddar Soup

Ingredients:

- 4 cups broccoli florets
- 1 medium onion, diced
- 2 cloves garlic, minced
- 4 cups chicken broth
- 2 cups shredded cheddar cheese
- 1 cup heavy cream
- 2 tablespoons butter
- 2 tablespoons flour
- Salt and freshly ground black pepper to taste

Instructions:

In a large pot, melt butter over medium heat. Add the onion and garlic, cooking until softened, about 5 minutes. Stir in the flour and cook for 2 minutes. Slowly add the chicken broth, stirring to prevent lumps. Bring to a boil and reduce to a simmer. Add the broccoli and cook until tender, about 10 minutes. Use an immersion blender to puree the soup slightly, leaving some broccoli chunks for texture. Stir in the heavy cream and shredded cheddar cheese, cooking until the cheese melts. Season with salt and pepper to taste. Serve warm.

Minestrone Soup

Ingredients:

- 2 tablespoons olive oil
- 1 medium onion, diced
- 2 carrots, diced
- 2 celery stalks, diced
- 2 cloves garlic, minced
- 1 zucchini, diced
- 1 cup green beans, chopped
- 1 can (14.5 oz) diced tomatoes
- 4 cups vegetable broth
- 1 cup pasta (small shells or elbow)
- 1 can (15 oz) kidney beans, drained and rinsed
- 1 teaspoon dried basil
- 1 teaspoon dried oregano
- Salt and freshly ground black pepper to taste
- Fresh parsley, for garnish

Instructions:

In a large pot, heat olive oil over medium heat. Add the onion, carrots, celery, and garlic, cooking until softened, about 5 minutes. Add the zucchini, green beans, diced tomatoes, vegetable broth, and pasta. Bring to a boil, then reduce the heat and simmer until the vegetables are tender and the pasta is cooked, about 15 minutes. Stir in the kidney beans, basil, oregano, salt, and pepper, and cook for another 5 minutes. Garnish with fresh parsley and serve hot.

Roasted Butternut Squash Soup

Ingredients:

- 1 medium butternut squash, peeled, seeded, and cubed
- 1 medium onion, diced
- 2 cloves garlic, minced
- 4 cups vegetable broth
- 1 teaspoon ground cumin
- 1 teaspoon ground ginger
- 1/2 cup coconut milk
- 2 tablespoons olive oil
- Salt and freshly ground black pepper to taste

Instructions:

Preheat the oven to 400°F (200°C). Toss the cubed butternut squash with olive oil, salt, and pepper, and spread in a single layer on a baking sheet. Roast for 25-30 minutes, or until tender. In a large pot, heat olive oil over medium heat and sauté the onion and garlic until softened. Add the roasted squash, vegetable broth, cumin, and ginger, bringing to a boil. Reduce heat and simmer for 10 minutes. Use an immersion blender to puree the soup until smooth. Stir in the coconut milk and adjust seasoning with salt and pepper. Serve warm.

Thai Coconut Chicken Soup

Ingredients:

- 2 tablespoons olive oil
- 1 lb chicken breast, thinly sliced
- 1 medium onion, diced
- 2 cloves garlic, minced
- 1-inch piece of fresh ginger, grated
- 2 cups coconut milk
- 2 cups chicken broth
- 1 tablespoon fish sauce
- 1 tablespoon lime juice
- 1/2 cup mushrooms, sliced
- 1 red bell pepper, sliced
- 2 tablespoons fresh cilantro, chopped
- 1-2 teaspoons red curry paste (optional)
- Salt and freshly ground black pepper to taste

Instructions:

In a large pot, heat olive oil over medium heat. Add the chicken slices and cook until browned. Remove the chicken and set aside. In the same pot, sauté the onion, garlic, and ginger until softened. Stir in the coconut milk, chicken broth, fish sauce, lime juice, mushrooms, bell pepper, and red curry paste. Bring to a boil, then reduce the heat and simmer for 10 minutes. Return the chicken to the pot and cook for an additional 5 minutes. Season with salt and pepper. Garnish with cilantro and serve hot.

Mushroom and Wild Rice Soup

Ingredients:

- 1 tablespoon olive oil
- 1 medium onion, diced
- 2 cloves garlic, minced
- 2 cups mushrooms, sliced
- 1/2 cup wild rice
- 4 cups vegetable broth
- 1 cup heavy cream
- 1 teaspoon fresh thyme, chopped
- Salt and freshly ground black pepper to taste

Instructions:

In a large pot, heat olive oil over medium heat. Add the onion and garlic, cooking until softened. Stir in the mushrooms and cook until they release their moisture, about 5 minutes. Add the wild rice and vegetable broth, and bring to a boil. Reduce the heat and simmer for 30-40 minutes, or until the rice is tender. Stir in the heavy cream and thyme, and cook for an additional 5 minutes. Season with salt and pepper to taste. Serve warm.

Italian Wedding Soup

Ingredients:

- 1/2 lb ground beef
- 1/2 lb ground pork
- 1/4 cup breadcrumbs
- 1/4 cup grated Parmesan cheese
- 1 egg, beaten
- 1 tablespoon fresh parsley, chopped
- 6 cups chicken broth
- 1 cup small pasta (like orzo or acini di pepe)
- 2 cups spinach, chopped
- Salt and freshly ground black pepper to taste

Instructions:

In a bowl, combine the ground beef, ground pork, breadcrumbs, Parmesan cheese, egg, parsley, salt, and pepper. Form the mixture into small meatballs, about 1 inch in diameter. In a large pot, bring the chicken broth to a boil. Add the meatballs and cook until they rise to the surface, about 10 minutes. Stir in the pasta and cook until al dente, about 8 minutes. Add the spinach and cook for another 2-3 minutes. Season with salt and pepper to taste. Serve warm.

Shrimp and Corn Chowder

Ingredients:

- 1 lb shrimp, peeled and deveined
- 2 cups corn kernels (fresh or frozen)
- 1 medium onion, diced
- 2 cloves garlic, minced
- 4 cups chicken broth
- 1 cup heavy cream
- 2 tablespoons butter
- 2 tablespoons flour
- Salt and freshly ground black pepper to taste
- Fresh parsley, for garnish

Instructions:

In a large pot, melt butter over medium heat. Add the onion and garlic, cooking until softened. Stir in the flour and cook for 2 minutes. Gradually add the chicken broth, stirring to prevent lumps. Bring to a simmer and cook for 10 minutes. Stir in the shrimp and corn, cooking until the shrimp turns pink, about 5 minutes. Add the heavy cream and cook for another 5 minutes. Season with salt and pepper to taste. Garnish with fresh parsley and serve.

Tuscan White Bean Soup

Ingredients:

- 2 tablespoons olive oil
- 1 medium onion, diced
- 2 cloves garlic, minced
- 2 cans (15 oz) white beans, drained and rinsed
- 4 cups vegetable broth
- 1 teaspoon dried rosemary
- 1/2 teaspoon dried thyme
- 1 cup kale, chopped
- Salt and freshly ground black pepper to taste

Instructions:

In a large pot, heat olive oil over medium heat. Add the onion and garlic, cooking until softened. Stir in the white beans, vegetable broth, rosemary, and thyme, and bring to a boil. Reduce the heat and simmer for 10 minutes. Add the kale and cook until wilted, about 5 minutes. Season with salt and pepper to taste. Serve warm.

Seafood Chowder

Ingredients:

- 1 lb mixed seafood (shrimp, scallops, clams)
- 1 medium onion, diced
- 2 cloves garlic, minced
- 2 cups potatoes, diced
- 4 cups seafood broth
- 1 cup heavy cream
- 2 tablespoons butter
- Salt and freshly ground black pepper to taste
- Fresh parsley, for garnish

Instructions:

In a large pot, melt butter over medium heat. Add the onion and garlic, cooking until softened. Add the potatoes and seafood broth, and bring to a boil. Reduce the heat and simmer until the potatoes are tender, about 10 minutes. Stir in the seafood and cook until just cooked through, about 5 minutes. Add the heavy cream and cook for another 5 minutes. Season with salt and pepper to taste. Garnish with fresh parsley and serve.

Sweet Potato and Carrot Soup

Ingredients:

- 2 medium sweet potatoes, peeled and cubed
- 3 carrots, peeled and chopped
- 1 medium onion, diced
- 2 cloves garlic, minced
- 4 cups vegetable broth
- 1 teaspoon ground cumin
- 1/2 teaspoon ground cinnamon
- 1/4 teaspoon ground nutmeg
- 1 tablespoon olive oil
- Salt and freshly ground black pepper to taste
- 1/2 cup coconut milk (optional)
- Fresh cilantro, for garnish

Instructions:

In a large pot, heat olive oil over medium heat. Add the onion and garlic, cooking until softened. Add the sweet potatoes, carrots, cumin, cinnamon, and nutmeg, and cook for another 5 minutes. Pour in the vegetable broth and bring to a boil. Reduce the heat and simmer for 20-25 minutes, or until the vegetables are tender. Use an immersion blender to puree the soup until smooth. Stir in the coconut milk if using, and season with salt and pepper to taste. Garnish with fresh cilantro and serve warm.

Roasted Cauliflower Soup

Ingredients:

- 1 medium head cauliflower, cut into florets
- 1 tablespoon olive oil
- 1 medium onion, diced
- 2 cloves garlic, minced
- 4 cups vegetable broth
- 1 teaspoon ground turmeric
- 1/2 teaspoon ground cumin
- Salt and freshly ground black pepper to taste
- 1/2 cup cream or coconut milk (optional)

Instructions:

Preheat the oven to 400°F (200°C). Toss the cauliflower florets with olive oil, salt, and pepper, and spread them on a baking sheet. Roast for 25-30 minutes, or until golden and tender. In a large pot, sauté the onion and garlic in olive oil over medium heat until softened. Add the roasted cauliflower, vegetable broth, turmeric, and cumin, and bring to a boil. Reduce heat and simmer for 10 minutes. Use an immersion blender to puree the soup until smooth. Stir in cream or coconut milk if desired, and season with salt and pepper. Serve warm.

Creamy Spinach and Artichoke Soup

Ingredients:

- 2 cups fresh spinach, chopped
- 1 can (14 oz) artichoke hearts, drained and chopped
- 1 medium onion, diced
- 2 cloves garlic, minced
- 4 cups vegetable broth
- 1 cup heavy cream
- 2 tablespoons olive oil
- 1 teaspoon lemon juice
- Salt and freshly ground black pepper to taste

Instructions:

In a large pot, heat olive oil over medium heat. Add the onion and garlic, cooking until softened. Stir in the chopped artichokes and cook for 2-3 minutes. Add the vegetable broth and bring to a boil. Reduce the heat and simmer for 10 minutes. Stir in the spinach and cook for another 5 minutes until wilted. Use an immersion blender to puree the soup until smooth. Add the heavy cream and lemon juice, and cook for another 5 minutes. Season with salt and pepper to taste. Serve warm.

Moroccan Chickpea Soup

Ingredients:

- 2 tablespoons olive oil
- 1 medium onion, diced
- 2 cloves garlic, minced
- 1 can (15 oz) chickpeas, drained and rinsed
- 1 can (14.5 oz) diced tomatoes
- 4 cups vegetable broth
- 1 teaspoon ground cumin
- 1 teaspoon ground coriander
- 1/2 teaspoon ground cinnamon
- 1/4 teaspoon ground turmeric
- 1/4 teaspoon ground paprika
- Salt and freshly ground black pepper to taste
- Fresh cilantro, for garnish

Instructions:

In a large pot, heat olive oil over medium heat. Add the onion and garlic, cooking until softened. Stir in the cumin, coriander, cinnamon, turmeric, and paprika, and cook for 1-2 minutes to release the spices' aroma. Add the chickpeas, diced tomatoes, and vegetable broth, and bring to a boil. Reduce the heat and simmer for 20 minutes. Use an immersion blender to partially puree the soup, leaving some texture. Season with salt and pepper to taste. Garnish with fresh cilantro and serve warm.

Tomato and Red Pepper Bisque

Ingredients:

- 4 medium tomatoes, diced
- 2 red bell peppers, chopped
- 1 medium onion, diced
- 2 cloves garlic, minced
- 3 cups vegetable broth
- 1 cup heavy cream
- 1 tablespoon olive oil
- 1 teaspoon dried thyme
- Salt and freshly ground black pepper to taste

Instructions:

In a large pot, heat olive oil over medium heat. Add the onion and garlic, cooking until softened. Stir in the tomatoes, red bell peppers, thyme, salt, and pepper, and cook for 10 minutes, until the vegetables soften. Add the vegetable broth and bring to a boil. Reduce the heat and simmer for 20 minutes. Use an immersion blender to puree the soup until smooth. Stir in the heavy cream and cook for another 5 minutes. Adjust seasoning with salt and pepper to taste. Serve warm.

Curried Lentil Soup

Ingredients:

- 1 tablespoon olive oil
- 1 medium onion, diced
- 2 cloves garlic, minced
- 1 cup dried red lentils, rinsed
- 1 can (14.5 oz) diced tomatoes
- 4 cups vegetable broth
- 1 tablespoon curry powder
- 1 teaspoon ground cumin
- 1/2 teaspoon ground turmeric
- Salt and freshly ground black pepper to taste
- Fresh cilantro, for garnish

Instructions:

In a large pot, heat olive oil over medium heat. Add the onion and garlic, cooking until softened. Stir in the curry powder, cumin, and turmeric, and cook for 1-2 minutes to release the spices' flavor. Add the lentils, diced tomatoes, and vegetable broth, and bring to a boil. Reduce the heat and simmer for 25-30 minutes, or until the lentils are tender. Season with salt and pepper to taste. Garnish with fresh cilantro and serve warm.

Chicken Tortilla Soup

Ingredients:

- 1 lb chicken breast, cooked and shredded
- 1 medium onion, diced
- 2 cloves garlic, minced
- 1 can (14.5 oz) diced tomatoes
- 4 cups chicken broth
- 1 teaspoon chili powder
- 1 teaspoon ground cumin
- 1/2 teaspoon paprika
- Salt and freshly ground black pepper to taste
- 1 cup corn kernels (fresh or frozen)
- 1/2 cup tortilla strips
- Fresh cilantro, for garnish

Instructions:

In a large pot, sauté the onion and garlic in olive oil over medium heat until softened. Stir in the chili powder, cumin, paprika, salt, and pepper, and cook for 1-2 minutes. Add the diced tomatoes, chicken broth, shredded chicken, and corn, and bring to a boil. Reduce the heat and simmer for 20 minutes. Serve the soup topped with tortilla strips and fresh cilantro.

Beef and Vegetable Soup

Ingredients:

- 1 lb beef stew meat, cubed
- 1 medium onion, diced
- 2 cloves garlic, minced
- 4 cups beef broth
- 1 cup carrots, chopped
- 1 cup celery, chopped
- 2 potatoes, diced
- 1 can (14.5 oz) diced tomatoes
- 1 teaspoon dried thyme
- Salt and freshly ground black pepper to taste

Instructions:

In a large pot, brown the beef stew meat over medium heat. Remove the beef and set aside. In the same pot, sauté the onion and garlic until softened. Stir in the beef broth, diced tomatoes, carrots, celery, potatoes, and thyme. Add the beef back to the pot and bring to a boil. Reduce heat and simmer for 45 minutes, or until the beef and vegetables are tender. Season with salt and pepper to taste. Serve warm.

Spicy Black Bean Soup

Ingredients:

- 2 tablespoons olive oil
- 1 medium onion, diced
- 2 cloves garlic, minced
- 2 cans (15 oz) black beans, drained and rinsed
- 4 cups vegetable broth
- 1 teaspoon ground cumin
- 1/2 teaspoon chili powder
- 1/4 teaspoon cayenne pepper (optional for extra heat)
- Salt and freshly ground black pepper to taste
- Fresh lime juice, for garnish
- Fresh cilantro, for garnish

Instructions:

In a large pot, heat olive oil over medium heat. Add the onion and garlic, cooking until softened. Stir in the cumin, chili powder, cayenne pepper, salt, and pepper, and cook for 1 minute. Add the black beans and vegetable broth, and bring to a boil. Reduce the heat and simmer for 20 minutes. Use an immersion blender to partially puree the soup, leaving some texture. Season with salt and pepper to taste. Garnish with lime juice and fresh cilantro before serving.

Pea and Mint Soup

Ingredients:

- 4 cups fresh or frozen peas
- 1 medium onion, diced
- 2 cloves garlic, minced
- 3 cups vegetable broth
- 1/2 cup heavy cream
- 1/4 cup fresh mint leaves
- 1 tablespoon olive oil
- Salt and freshly ground black pepper to taste

Instructions:

In a large pot, heat olive oil over medium heat. Add the onion and garlic, cooking until softened. Add the peas and vegetable broth, and bring to a boil. Reduce the heat and simmer for 10 minutes. Remove from heat and stir in the fresh mint leaves. Use an immersion blender to puree the soup until smooth. Stir in the heavy cream, and season with salt and pepper to taste. Serve warm, garnished with additional mint leaves if desired.

Pumpkin Soup with Ginger

Ingredients:

- 4 cups pumpkin, peeled and cubed
- 1 medium onion, diced
- 2 cloves garlic, minced
- 1 tablespoon fresh ginger, grated
- 4 cups vegetable broth
- 1/2 cup coconut milk
- 1 tablespoon olive oil
- 1/2 teaspoon ground cinnamon
- Salt and freshly ground black pepper to taste

Instructions:

In a large pot, heat olive oil over medium heat. Add the onion, garlic, and ginger, cooking until fragrant. Add the pumpkin cubes, cinnamon, salt, and pepper, and cook for 5 minutes. Pour in the vegetable broth and bring to a boil. Reduce the heat and simmer for 20 minutes, or until the pumpkin is tender. Use an immersion blender to puree the soup until smooth. Stir in the coconut milk and adjust seasoning as needed. Serve warm.

Baked Potato Soup

Ingredients:

- 4 large baking potatoes, cooked and cubed
- 1 medium onion, diced
- 2 cloves garlic, minced
- 4 cups chicken broth
- 1 cup heavy cream
- 1 cup shredded cheddar cheese
- 4 slices bacon, cooked and crumbled
- 1 tablespoon olive oil
- Salt and freshly ground black pepper to taste
- Chopped green onions, for garnish

Instructions:

In a large pot, heat olive oil over medium heat. Add the onion and garlic, cooking until softened. Stir in the chicken broth and cubed potatoes, and bring to a boil. Reduce heat and simmer for 10 minutes. Use an immersion blender to partially puree the soup, leaving some chunks for texture. Stir in the heavy cream and shredded cheddar cheese until melted. Season with salt and pepper to taste. Serve topped with crumbled bacon and green onions.

Chicken and Rice Soup

Ingredients:

- 1 lb cooked chicken breast, shredded
- 1 medium onion, diced
- 2 carrots, diced
- 2 celery stalks, diced
- 1 cup long-grain rice
- 6 cups chicken broth
- 1 tablespoon olive oil
- Salt and freshly ground black pepper to taste

Instructions:

In a large pot, heat olive oil over medium heat. Add the onion, carrots, and celery, cooking until softened. Stir in the chicken broth and bring to a boil. Add the rice and cook for 15-20 minutes, or until the rice is tender. Stir in the shredded chicken and cook for another 5 minutes. Season with salt and pepper to taste. Serve warm.

Chicken and Wild Rice Soup

Ingredients:

- 1 lb cooked chicken breast, shredded
- 1 medium onion, diced
- 2 carrots, diced
- 2 celery stalks, diced
- 1 cup wild rice, cooked
- 6 cups chicken broth
- 1/2 cup heavy cream
- 1 tablespoon olive oil
- Salt and freshly ground black pepper to taste

Instructions:

In a large pot, heat olive oil over medium heat. Add the onion, carrots, and celery, cooking until softened. Stir in the chicken broth and bring to a boil. Add the cooked wild rice and shredded chicken, and simmer for 10 minutes. Stir in the heavy cream and adjust seasoning with salt and pepper. Serve warm.

Roasted Garlic and Potato Soup

Ingredients:

- 1 head of garlic, roasted
- 4 large potatoes, peeled and cubed
- 1 medium onion, diced
- 4 cups vegetable broth
- 1 cup heavy cream
- 1 tablespoon olive oil
- Salt and freshly ground black pepper to taste
- Fresh chives, for garnish

Instructions:

Preheat oven to 400°F (200°C). Cut the top off the garlic head, drizzle with olive oil, wrap in foil, and roast for 30 minutes. In a large pot, heat olive oil over medium heat. Add the onion, cooking until softened. Stir in the potatoes and vegetable broth, and bring to a boil. Reduce heat and simmer for 20 minutes, or until potatoes are tender. Squeeze the roasted garlic into the soup and use an immersion blender to puree until smooth. Stir in the heavy cream and season with salt and pepper. Garnish with fresh chives and serve warm.

Creamy Cauliflower Soup

Ingredients:

- 1 medium head of cauliflower, cut into florets
- 1 medium onion, diced
- 2 cloves garlic, minced
- 4 cups vegetable broth
- 1/2 cup heavy cream
- 1 tablespoon olive oil
- Salt and freshly ground black pepper to taste
- Shredded Parmesan cheese, for garnish

Instructions:

In a large pot, heat olive oil over medium heat. Add the onion and garlic, cooking until softened. Stir in the cauliflower florets and vegetable broth, and bring to a boil. Reduce heat and simmer for 20 minutes, or until the cauliflower is tender. Use an immersion blender to puree the soup until smooth. Stir in the heavy cream and adjust seasoning with salt and pepper. Garnish with Parmesan cheese and serve warm.

Kale and White Bean Soup

Ingredients:

- 2 cups kale, chopped
- 1 can (15 oz) white beans, drained and rinsed
- 1 medium onion, diced
- 2 carrots, diced
- 4 cups vegetable broth
- 1 tablespoon olive oil
- 1/2 teaspoon dried thyme
- Salt and freshly ground black pepper to taste

Instructions:

In a large pot, heat olive oil over medium heat. Add the onion and carrots, cooking until softened. Stir in the vegetable broth, white beans, and thyme, and bring to a boil. Reduce heat and simmer for 15 minutes. Add the chopped kale and cook for another 5 minutes, or until tender. Season with salt and pepper to taste. Serve warm.

Sweet Corn and Zucchini Soup

Ingredients:

- 3 cups fresh or frozen sweet corn kernels
- 2 medium zucchinis, diced
- 1 medium onion, diced
- 2 cloves garlic, minced
- 4 cups vegetable broth
- 1/2 cup heavy cream
- 1 tablespoon olive oil
- Salt and freshly ground black pepper to taste
- Fresh parsley, for garnish

Instructions:

In a large pot, heat olive oil over medium heat. Add the onion and garlic, cooking until softened. Stir in the zucchini and cook for 5 minutes. Add the corn and vegetable broth, and bring to a boil. Reduce heat and simmer for 15 minutes. Use an immersion blender to puree the soup partially, leaving some texture. Stir in the heavy cream, season with salt and pepper, and garnish with parsley before serving.

Roasted Beetroot Soup

Ingredients:

- 4 medium beets, peeled and diced
- 1 medium onion, diced
- 2 cloves garlic, minced
- 4 cups vegetable broth
- 1/2 cup coconut milk
- 1 tablespoon olive oil
- 1 tablespoon apple cider vinegar
- Salt and freshly ground black pepper to taste
- Sour cream or Greek yogurt, for garnish

Instructions:

Preheat oven to 400°F (200°C). Toss the diced beets with olive oil and roast for 30-35 minutes until tender. In a large pot, sauté the onion and garlic until softened. Add the roasted beets and vegetable broth, bringing to a boil. Reduce heat and simmer for 10 minutes. Use an immersion blender to puree the soup until smooth. Stir in the coconut milk and apple cider vinegar, adjusting seasoning as needed. Serve garnished with sour cream or Greek yogurt.

Cabbage and Sausage Soup

Ingredients:

- 1/2 head green cabbage, shredded
- 1 lb smoked sausage, sliced
- 1 medium onion, diced
- 2 carrots, diced
- 4 cups chicken broth
- 1 tablespoon olive oil
- Salt and freshly ground black pepper to taste
- Fresh dill, for garnish

Instructions:

In a large pot, heat olive oil over medium heat. Add the sausage slices and cook until browned. Remove and set aside. In the same pot, sauté the onion and carrots until softened. Add the cabbage and cook for 5 minutes. Pour in the chicken broth, add the sausage, and simmer for 20 minutes. Season with salt and pepper to taste. Garnish with fresh dill before serving.

Spicy Pumpkin and Lentil Soup

Ingredients:

- 4 cups pumpkin, peeled and cubed
- 1 cup red lentils, rinsed
- 1 medium onion, diced
- 2 cloves garlic, minced
- 1 tablespoon curry powder
- 4 cups vegetable broth
- 1/2 cup coconut milk
- 1 tablespoon olive oil
- Salt and freshly ground black pepper to taste

Instructions:

In a large pot, heat olive oil over medium heat. Sauté the onion and garlic until fragrant. Stir in the curry powder, cooking for 1 minute. Add the pumpkin, lentils, and vegetable broth, bringing to a boil. Reduce heat and simmer for 25 minutes, or until the pumpkin and lentils are tender. Use an immersion blender to puree the soup until smooth. Stir in the coconut milk and adjust seasoning as needed. Serve warm.

Italian Sausage and Kale Soup

Ingredients:

- 1 lb Italian sausage, crumbled
- 2 cups kale, chopped
- 1 medium onion, diced
- 2 cloves garlic, minced
- 4 cups chicken broth
- 1/2 cup heavy cream
- 1 tablespoon olive oil
- Salt and freshly ground black pepper to taste

Instructions:

In a large pot, heat olive oil over medium heat. Cook the sausage until browned, then remove and set aside. In the same pot, sauté the onion and garlic until softened. Add the chicken broth and bring to a boil. Stir in the kale and cooked sausage, simmering for 10 minutes. Stir in the heavy cream and season with salt and pepper. Serve warm.

Smoky Ham and Potato Soup

Ingredients:

- 1 lb ham, diced
- 4 medium potatoes, peeled and cubed
- 1 medium onion, diced
- 2 cloves garlic, minced
- 4 cups chicken broth
- 1/2 teaspoon smoked paprika
- 1 cup heavy cream
- 1 tablespoon olive oil
- Salt and freshly ground black pepper to taste

Instructions:

In a large pot, heat olive oil over medium heat. Sauté the onion and garlic until softened. Add the potatoes, smoked paprika, and chicken broth, bringing to a boil. Reduce heat and simmer for 15 minutes, or until the potatoes are tender. Stir in the diced ham and heavy cream, cooking for another 5 minutes. Season with salt and pepper to taste. Serve warm.

Clam and Bacon Chowder

Ingredients:

- 4 slices bacon, diced
- 1 lb fresh clams, cleaned
- 2 medium potatoes, peeled and diced
- 1 medium onion, diced
- 2 cloves garlic, minced
- 4 cups seafood broth
- 1 cup heavy cream
- 1 tablespoon olive oil
- Salt and freshly ground black pepper to taste
- Fresh parsley, for garnish

Instructions:

In a large pot, cook the diced bacon until crispy. Remove and set aside. In the same pot, sauté the onion and garlic until softened. Add the potatoes and seafood broth, bringing to a boil. Reduce heat and simmer for 15 minutes, or until the potatoes are tender. Stir in the clams and cook until they open, discarding any that remain closed. Add the heavy cream and crispy bacon, seasoning with salt and pepper. Garnish with parsley before serving.

Coconut Curry Butternut Squash Soup

Ingredients:

- 1 medium butternut squash, peeled and cubed
- 1 medium onion, diced
- 2 cloves garlic, minced
- 1 tablespoon curry powder
- 1/2 teaspoon ground ginger
- 1 can (13.5 oz) coconut milk
- 4 cups vegetable broth
- 1 tablespoon olive oil
- Salt and freshly ground black pepper to taste
- Fresh cilantro, for garnish

Instructions:

Heat olive oil in a large pot over medium heat. Sauté the onion and garlic until softened. Add the curry powder and ginger, cooking for 1 minute. Stir in the squash, coconut milk, and vegetable broth. Bring to a boil, then reduce heat and simmer for 20 minutes, or until the squash is tender. Blend the soup until smooth, season with salt and pepper, and garnish with cilantro before serving.

Vietnamese Pho

Ingredients:

- 8 cups beef or chicken broth
- 1 large onion, halved
- 3-inch piece of ginger, sliced
- 2 star anise pods
- 1 cinnamon stick
- 1 lb rice noodles
- 1 lb thinly sliced beef or chicken
- Fresh basil, cilantro, and mint leaves
- Bean sprouts, lime wedges, and sliced chili peppers for serving

Instructions:

In a large pot, bring the broth to a simmer. Add the onion, ginger, star anise, and cinnamon, and simmer for 30 minutes. Strain the broth and return it to the pot. Cook the rice noodles according to package instructions. Place noodles in bowls, top with the beef or chicken, and pour hot broth over. Serve with fresh herbs, bean sprouts, lime, and chili peppers.

Fish Chowder

Ingredients:

- 1 lb firm white fish (e.g., cod or haddock), cubed
- 2 medium potatoes, diced
- 1 medium onion, diced
- 2 cups seafood broth
- 1 cup heavy cream
- 1 tablespoon butter
- Salt and freshly ground black pepper to taste
- Fresh parsley, for garnish

Instructions:

In a pot, melt butter over medium heat and sauté the onion until softened. Add the potatoes and seafood broth, simmering until the potatoes are tender. Stir in the fish and cook for 5-7 minutes, or until the fish is cooked through. Add the heavy cream, season with salt and pepper, and garnish with parsley before serving.

Potato Leek Soup

Ingredients:

- 4 medium potatoes, peeled and diced
- 2 large leeks, sliced and washed
- 4 cups vegetable or chicken broth
- 1 cup heavy cream
- 2 tablespoons butter
- Salt and freshly ground black pepper to taste
- Chopped chives, for garnish

Instructions:

Melt butter in a pot over medium heat. Sauté the leeks until softened. Add the potatoes and broth, bringing to a boil. Reduce heat and simmer until the potatoes are tender. Blend the soup until smooth, stir in the cream, and season with salt and pepper. Garnish with chives before serving.

Eggplant and Tomato Soup

Ingredients:

- 1 large eggplant, diced
- 4 medium tomatoes, diced
- 1 medium onion, diced
- 2 cloves garlic, minced
- 4 cups vegetable broth
- 1 tablespoon olive oil
- Salt and freshly ground black pepper to taste
- Fresh basil, for garnish

Instructions:

Heat olive oil in a pot over medium heat. Sauté the onion and garlic until softened. Add the eggplant and cook for 5 minutes. Stir in the tomatoes and vegetable broth, bringing to a boil. Reduce heat and simmer for 20 minutes. Blend the soup until smooth, season with salt and pepper, and garnish with basil.

Chicken and Sweet Potato Soup

Ingredients:

- 1 lb chicken breast, diced
- 2 medium sweet potatoes, cubed
- 1 medium onion, diced
- 2 cloves garlic, minced
- 4 cups chicken broth
- 1 teaspoon paprika
- 1 tablespoon olive oil
- Salt and freshly ground black pepper to taste

Instructions:

Heat olive oil in a pot over medium heat. Cook the chicken until browned and set aside. In the same pot, sauté the onion and garlic until softened. Add the sweet potatoes, chicken broth, and paprika, bringing to a boil. Reduce heat and simmer until the sweet potatoes are tender. Return the chicken to the pot, season with salt and pepper, and serve warm.

Green Bean and Ham Soup

Ingredients:

- 1 lb green beans, trimmed and cut
- 1 lb ham, diced
- 2 medium potatoes, diced
- 1 medium onion, diced
- 4 cups chicken broth
- Salt and freshly ground black pepper to taste

Instructions:

In a pot, combine the ham, potatoes, onion, and chicken broth. Bring to a boil, then reduce heat and simmer for 10 minutes. Add the green beans and cook for an additional 10 minutes, or until the vegetables are tender. Season with salt and pepper and serve warm.

Coconut Lentil Soup

Ingredients:

- 1 cup red lentils, rinsed
- 1 can (13.5 oz) coconut milk
- 4 cups vegetable broth
- 1 medium onion, diced
- 2 cloves garlic, minced
- 1 tablespoon curry powder
- 1 tablespoon olive oil
- Salt and freshly ground black pepper to taste

Instructions:

Heat olive oil in a pot over medium heat. Sauté the onion and garlic until softened. Stir in the curry powder, cooking for 1 minute. Add the lentils, coconut milk, and vegetable broth, bringing to a boil. Reduce heat and simmer for 20 minutes, or until the lentils are tender. Season with salt and pepper and serve warm.

www.ingramcontent.com/pod-product-compliance
Lightning Source LLC
LaVergne TN
LVHW081507060526
838201LV00056BA/2992